Money Magic for Beginners

Analyses, Methods, Invocations and Rituals

Contact: www.HarryEilenstein.de
Harry.Eilenstein@web.de
Harry Eilenstein at youtube

Production and publishing house: BoD – Books on Demand, Norderstedt

ISBN: 9783753473222

Table of Contents

I The Essence of Money

In magic it is like everywhere else in life: Clarity about what is important to oneself is beneficial. Therefore, even if you are short of money (which is probably the reason for buying this book), you should first take a closer look at what money actually is. That, what one knows, is easier to obtain – and against an enemy, whom one knows, one can fight more easily. Well – it will become clear whether money is a friend or an enemy ... or something completely different ...

So far, five epochs can be distinguished in relation to money, although the fifth epoch has just begun – so only the first four epochs are really known.

Paleolithic Age
(until 10,500 B.C.)

In the Paleolithic people lived together in clans of 12-30 people. Everyone in this clan was dependent on everyone else – just like in today's families. This means that everyone contributed what they could for the prosperity of the clan, and in turn got what they needed from the clan. One had what one had hunted, gathered, built or created together. The clan had to do and obtain everything they needed to survive. The clan was a "communal self-provider."

Neolithic Age
(10,500-3,250 B.C.)

In the Neolithic period, people began farming and raising livestock, which was so effective that 500 times more people could now live together than before. This led, among other things, to specializations in activities and to the first professions. This necessitated bartering – the farmer gave the stonemason a sack of flour for a well-sharpened axe of stone.

It was also at this time that the first traders emerged who brought coveted goods from specialists to distant places – these could be, for example, the particularly sharp stone tools that stonemasons had made in a place where Obisidian was found.

Kingship
(3250 B.C. - 1500 A.D.)

Through kingship, the work of the people in very large areas was centrally controlled and coordinated, making the work of the people much more effective. This coordination was most important in irrigation.

Due to the once again significantly increased number of people living together at that time, due to the more and more differentiated professions, as well as due to the "abstract work" of the administration, the army, the scribes, the artisans, the temple builders, etc., who did not directly produce consumer goods, barter was no longer sufficient to coordinate the activities in a kingdom.

It was therefore necessary to value the individual activities. To do this, one first used a widely used commodity such as bread and the like as a yardstick in which to express the value of all products and activities. A hoe was worth five loaves, a chicken seven loaves, an egg a quarter of bread, etc.

Widely available but perishable products could be used to value other products but they could not be stored as value – such as a warehouse full of stone tools. For this reason one chose other more permanent things such as hides or shells, which became eventually the standard of valuation.

Since a skin also has a value in itself, but a shell does not, there was the problem that everyone could look for shells on the beach and exchange them for something else – so the first inflation was born … Therefore, people looked for something durable but rare that could be used as a measure of value and unit of exchange. That's how they finally came up with gold.

Since it was tedious to have to weigh and possibly cut a gold piece for each trade, because it was too big, one went over to casting the gold pieces in certain sizes, with which one could then count the price (value) of the commodity. This is how the first coins were created.

It was also at this time that the markets were founded, that is, the central places where everyone came together who had made something and wanted to exchange it for something else. In the simple bartering in the Neolithic period there was no market – at that time you went to the man in the village who had chickens, for example, and asked him what he would exchange one of his chickens for.

Materialism
(1500-1950 AD)

Due to research, inventions, and industrialization, materialism had many more goods than ever before. However, new, large structures also emerged: for example, the factory took the place of the craftsman.

These large structures made the money system more susceptible to fluctuations of all kinds: goods could be made more expensive (if you had the best ones); wages could be lowered (if there were more workers than labor); the introduction of paper money meant that the state could print money to finance a war (this also led to inflation), and so on.

Moreover, activities began to be oriented more and more towards money instead of goods: Inferior goods were produced; short-lived products were manufactured so that customers would soon have to buy new ones; tenements were built in which their owners would not have wanted to live; etc.

Furthermore, people began to trade in property rights, i.e. shares, securities, government bonds, and the like. People no longer bought goods, but shares in the access to the profit created by the production of goods. These money transactions increased more and more, so that they finally made up more than 80% of all transactions that existed in a national economy. So 80% of all contracts were only about money and no longer about goods. Money had developed a life of its own …

Globalization
(since 1950 AD)

Since the end of the Second World War it became obvious to the people that the development dynamics generally existing at that time could not continue in such a way: World wars, atomic bomb, overpopulation, limited raw materials, environmental pollution, extinction of species, etc.

Since then, a new way of dealing with each other and with the earth as a whole has been sought. A stable system is needed, which prevents that humans on earth exterminate themselves. There is little point in discussing the advantages and disadvantages of globalization – because the atomic bomb, overpopulation, climate change, environmental destruction, etc. have led to a interdependence, which is very real. The question is how to deal with it.

A necessary innovation here is that until now the individual and also a culture or a people defined itself by its border – which no longer works in a globalized overall culture. The individual and the people must find their own identity in their own quality instead of in their border. So a concept is needed that takes into account both globalization and the individuality of the individual or a culture.

Globalization also leads to the fact that it becomes necessary for the individual to be carried in trust by the whole and in turn to carry the whole in responsibility. Thus, a continuum, a large family of individuals, is emerging.

What does this mean for money?

If money is what everyone strives for, there can be no peaceful globalization, because then the struggle for money blocks the view of the thing itself. It is therefore necessary that the economic mode and the money change in such a way that it is again obvious that money in itself has no value, but that it is a tool, a means to an end, a standard of valuation.

- - -

This small overview should show above all that in life it is never primarily about money, but about needs, which one wants to fulfill – and for this one tries nowadays first of all to procure sufficiently money. This money fixation leads to the problems just described.

The design of a meaningful money-magic, which takes into account the present situation of us humans on earth, is therefore somewhat more complex and multi-layered than the simple question "How do I get a lot of money?"

II   Classical Forms of Money Magic

There are quite a number of traditional methods in magic to get money. The most famous of all money magic is certainly the philosopher's stone, which turns lead into gold. However, this philosopher's stone is very speculative – the only way in which research for the stone has made an alchemist rich has been the accidental invention of porcelain in the search for the philosopher's stone.

But even leaving aside this rather speculative method, there are still several different ways of making money by magic.

II 1.   Earth Talisman

The four elements are the four things people are generally interested in – when someone goes to a fortuneteller, they almost always want to know about money, love and health. These are exactly the four elements:

Earth   = Money
Water   = Love
Fire   = Health
Air   = Knowledge

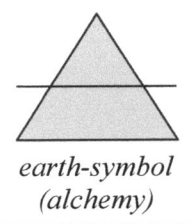

earth-symbol (alchemy)

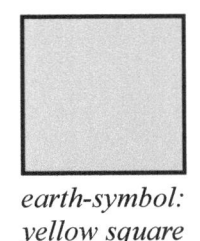

earth-symbol: yellow square (India)

So you can make and consecrate an earth talisman to get money.

There are two important symbols for the earth – one comes from alchemy, the other from the Indian meditation tradition.

For an earth talisman, one can cut such a symbol out of clay, saw it out of metal, chisel it out of stone, and so on. The production of a square is more obvious in this case, because the protruding lines of the alchemical symbol are difficult to make stable.

On one side of this square, earth symbols such as the alchemical symbol are engraved, and on the other side, a request to the earth is written in a short statement, such as "Wealth" or "Prosperity for my family" or similar.

The consecration of the talisman consists in asking the earth element, an earth deity or the earth beings ("dwarves") to give power to this talisman and to fulfill the wish.

One can also draw the invoking earth pentagram over the

talisman and ask the earth archangel Auriel for help. Auriel is traditionally imagined in the colors of lemon yellow, reddish brown, olive green and black. He stands against a background of fields, pastures, gardens and forests. The invoking earth pentagram is drawn in the air with index and middle finger as in the sketch below and imagined. Thereby one sings (intones, vibrates) the two names "Agla" and "Auriel".

In the "classical" occidental magic the element earth is assigned to the north, which can be included in this ritual.

At the end you put this talisman on the house altar or bury it in a powerful place in the earth or similar.

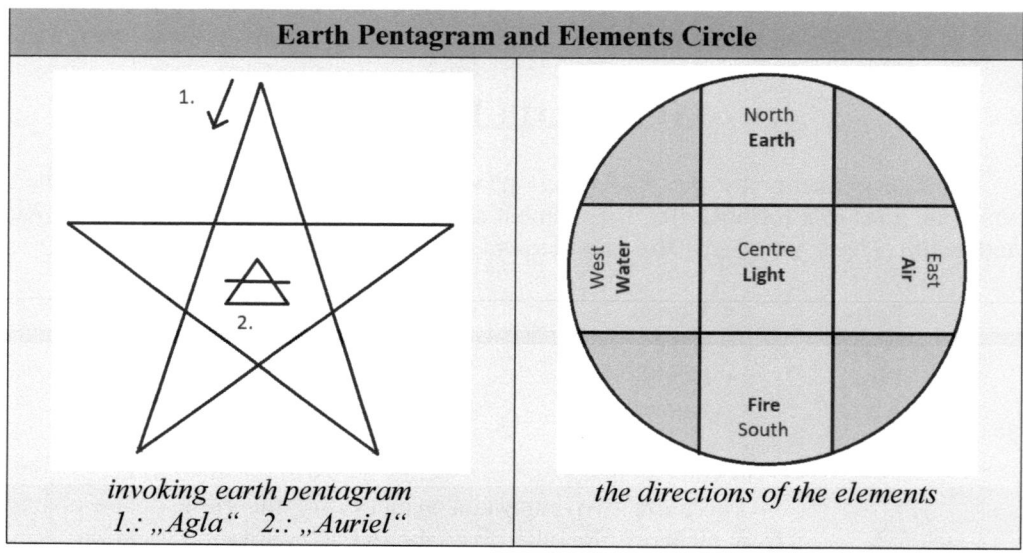

Earth Pentagram and Elements Circle
invoking earth pentagram 1.: „Agla" 2.: „Auriel"	the directions of the elements

II 2.   Jupiter Talisman

Jupiter

In astrology, Jupiter is the planet responsible for abundance and wealth. To him belong the number "4", accordingly also the square, furthermore the metal tin and Thursday. So on a Thursday you can cut out a square disk of tin and engrave Jupiter symbols on one side and your own wish on the other side.

Among the better known symbols is the planetary symbol itself and the square of numbers. This square contains four times four fields (Jupiter number), in which the numbers from 1 to 16 are arranged in such a way that each row, each column and each diagonal always has the sum 34.

seal of Jupiter

Other symbols such as the "Seal of Jupiter" have also been derived from this field.

This talisman is also consecrated by asking Jupiter to give power to this talisman and to fulfill the wish written on it.

One can extend such a consecration in all ways that are congenial to oneself: by the Lesser Pentagram Ritual as an introduction, by burning Jupiter incense, by a blue cloth on the altar and blue candles (Jupiter's color), and so on.

4	14	15	1
9	7	6	12
5	11	10	8
16	2	3	13

square of Jupiter

One can also draw the hexagram of Jupiter over the talisman four times in succession (Jupiter number), chanting the Jupiter names.

While drawing the two triangles in the air over the talisman with the index and middle fingers (1st and 2nd line in the sketch on the left: hexagram), chant the God name "El".

While drawing the Jupiter symbol in the center (3rd line: symbol) one chants the word "Ararita".

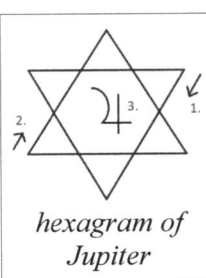

hexagram of Jupiter

The important point here is that all the tools have mainly the function to increase the concentration of the magician or the witch.

This talisman is also afterwards either placed on the altar or buried in the ground.

II 3. Mantra

Instead of making and consecrating a talisman, one can also use a mantra – it is simply a question of whether one is more the ritual type or the meditative type.

The two words of the mantra you use correspond to the two sides of the talisman: the first word is the name of the deity you are addressing (symbols on the talisman); the second word corresponds to the phrase (wish) on the other side of the talisman.

Thus, a Jupiter mantra could be "Jupiter – Prosperity." Since prosperity and possessions belong among the chakras to the Hara, this mantra can be related to the Hara. So this mantra meditation would look like this:

1. a) inhale
   b) imagination: inhale light and direct it into the Hara
   c) speak "Jupiter" inwardly

2. a) exhale
   b) imagination: let the light radiate from the Hara into the surroundings
   c) speak inwardly "prosperity"

The imagined light can be imagined as either white (neutral) or blue (Jupiter).

For this mantra to work, one should speak it daily for at least a few weeks. It is not possible to give more precise times for the duration of the daily meditation and for the number of weeks, because this is different for each person.

II 4. Invocation of the Gods

Another approach is to turn directly to a deity of prosperity such as Jupiter among the Romans, Freyr and Njörd among the Germanic tribes, the Indian Lakshmi, and so on.

It is useful to know a little about the deity in question if you want to ask him or her for help. The arrangement of this request is again very individual: the Lesser Pentagram Ritual as an introduction, a statue of the deity in question, incense, symbols on the altar, candles, ritual garb, etc.

The central element is addressing the deity and making the request. This can be a short sentence or a longer speech, it can have been formulated beforehand or improvised – it should be kept as it feels good.

It is not absolutely necessary, but quite beneficial, to imagine the deity in front of you while speaking to it.

It is also possible, to do this ritual only inwards as a meditation – this depends on the individual style.

II 5. Sacrifice

A traditional method is also "bartering with the gods": one tells the gods that one will now cut off one's hair, for example, and receive prosperity in return. In the past, one used to sacrifice a chicken, for example, in such a context. Among the North American prairie Indians it is customary to sacrifice some of one's own blood, because they believe that only one's own body really belongs to oneself.

The sacrificial method is quite effective, but actually superfluous – the gods do not need sacrifices and are happy to give even without a gift in return.

This method works especially well if one believes that the world is a place of scarcity – for then barter is the obvious method of obtaining something from another.

The sacrifice of a few drops of one's own blood in a ritual, of course, increases one's concentration quite significantly – and also impresses upon one's subconscious mind the importance of the request in question to the deities.

The concrete execution of the sacrifice-method depends again an the individual preferences and aversions.

13

II 6.   Sigil-Magic

Sigil magic is in a way the counterpart of sacrificial magic: Here only the will of the magician counts and nothing else.

The short sentence, which expresses what one wants, is first transformed into a sigil. Afterwards the magician concentrates once intensively on this Sigil and "sends" it thereby out – then the sigil "brings" the desired to the magician. The concentration during the "sending off" can be obtained by pain, desire, disgust or also simply by a high, aid-free concentration ability.

The transformation of the sentence into a sigil proceeds in three steps:

1. The letters in the sentence "I am rich." are reduced by deleting double letters. This then leaves "I am rch" remains, i.e. "iamrch." Mostly, however, one uses the capital letters: "IAMRCH".

2. These letters are now written on top and beside of each other, so that a "letter pattern" or a "letter cluster" is created.

3. This "letter pattern" is simplified until a memorable sigil is formed. This sigill may also by its form radiate richness and stability.

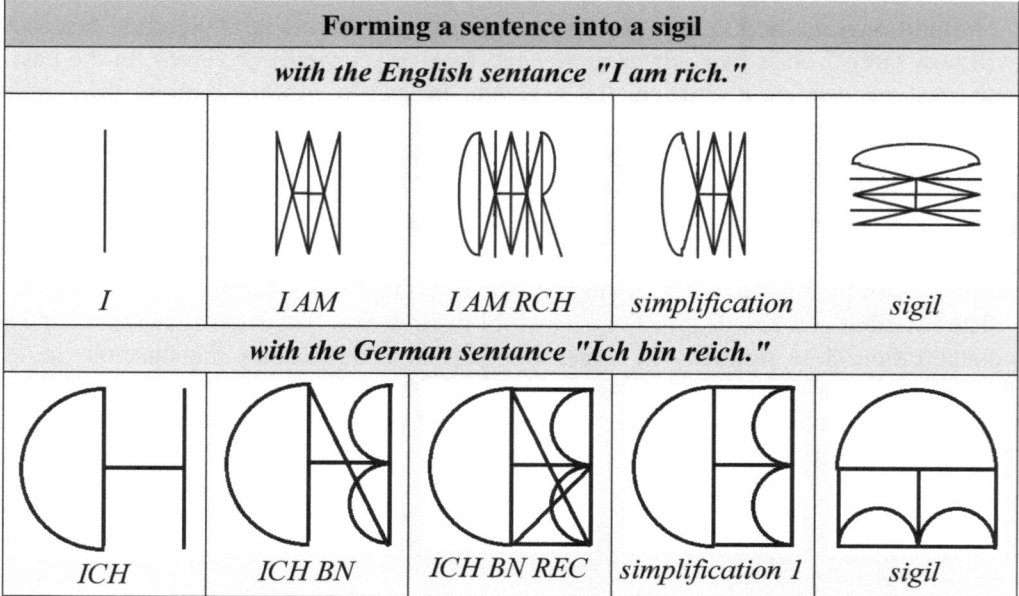

Forming a sentence into a sigil				
with the English sentence "I am rich."				
I	*I AM*	*I AM RCH*	*simplification*	*sigil*
with the German sentance "Ich bin reich."				
ICH	*ICH BN*	*ICH BN REC*	*simplification 1*	*sigil*

II 7. Auto-Suggestion

There are many methods for autohypnosis or autosuggestion. For a while, writing the wish on the soles of one's shoes, which is thus then spread, so to speak, throughout the world, has been quite popular.

But there is no limit to creativity here:

- 20 pieces of paper with the wish phrase, distributed in the apartment at clearly visible place;
- a gold coin in one's wallet;
- a mantra that one always speaks;
- giving away the change one receives to represent prosperity;
- a coin that one draws in the palm of one's hand or on one's thumbnail;
  etc.

II 8. Dream Journeys

If the chosen method has worked already and you are rich by now, you can stop reading here and enjoy life ... if not, it is recommended to continue reading.

If you have not had any success, it is advisable to see if you can see the cause for this failure: self-sabotage, doubt, poverty complex, etc.?

If the reason is not obvious, it can be helpful to make a dream journey to the topic "money" or to make a dream journey to Jupiter and to ask him, what helps most effectively on one's way to prosperity.

There is hardly a dream journey, on which one does not experience something, which one did not know or recognize before – therefore these dream journeys are actually almost always worthwhile themselves.

III An Eye-Opening Money Game

The shaman Francesca Boring from the Indian tribe of the Shoshone showed me several years ago a very practical method with which one can recognize the basic situation with a topic from one's own life.

For this method you need a helper. It is beneficial, but not absolutely necessary, that both already have experience with family constellations.

In the context of the money theme of this book, the "money-seeker" would stand for himself – the helper, on the other hand, embodies the money.

Both stand in the room like in a family constellation and follow the movement impulses they have. From time to time, both pause and briefly tell each other what they are feeling. Then they move on intuitively.

Possibly the money flees from the money-seeker … or it makes itself small and hides … or it attacks the money-seeker … or it just stands around apathetically … or it is sad and depressed …

The money-seeker can also show (and feel) very different behaviors: greed … fear … shyness … joy … reluctance … maybe he even flees away from the money ….

The interaction of the money and the money-seeker is very revealing – and often so drastic and obvious and amusing that both have to laugh.

Possibly it turns out that the money-seeker thinks money is dirty and immoral. Or he thinks money is power – and he himself acts usually the victim role and therefore fears power. Or he associates money with painful work. Or he has such poor self-esteem that he believes he is not entitled to hace any money. Or he may very effectively desire wealth for others, but not for himself at all.

There are many ways in which the previous biography of the money-seeker has shaped his relationship to money.

Often money does not start to flow in one's life until such an old imprinting has been dissolved.

IV An Alternative

At this point the short history of money from the first chapter comes into play: Why does one want to perform a money spell? To get money, of course. But what does one need the money for? After all, money is not an end in itself.

The general view of money leads to the fact that there is a very widespread competition for money – (almost) everybody wants to have as much of it as possible … This makes money a scarcity object, over which everybody fights.

It doesn't look very sensible to fight for it – except if you think you can be stronger than all the others. That is already by definition a recipe that can work only for one – just the winner in this fight. Just as there can be only one javelin world champion. Not very effective for all mankind …

So you could hava look whether you can find another way to your own goal. There is at least the possibility to wish not for money, but for example for the bicycle, which one wants to buy for the money. The probability that one gets 200€ as a present is not very large – the probability that someone has bought a new bicycle and would give away his old one is obviously much greater.

If you wish for the concrete things you need, the situation is much more relaxed. And if you get enough things this way that you would otherwise have to spend a lot of money to buy, you end up with enough money for everything you need.

This "wanting things" doesn't mean at all that you only get old junk – I got all my home furnishings (including keybord, harp, congas and PC), my e-bike and quite a few more this way. I also have only old, stylish furniture that even match exactly in style, even though they came from different sources.

If you ask life for the appropriate things that you need, life (or God or chance or whatever you want to call it) may well send you things that you can be happy about and that are not just a stopgap.

V   Money Magic and Astrology

V 1.   General

In a way, of course, all planets always have to do with all subjects, even if Jupiter is the most important in the money subject. In the case of money, the planets may have the following tasks:

- Moon: material basis of security
- Mercury: skill, trade, negotiations
- Venus: charm
- Sun: self-confidence
- Mars: energy, work, struggle
- Jupiter: abundance, prosperity, enjoyment, organization
- Saturn: preservation, constancy, inheritance
- Uranus: serendipity, invention
- Neptune: confidence in life
- Pluto: single-mindedness to the goal

If you can see that one of this points is the centre of your trouble with money, it would be helpful to ask the relevant planet for help, to make a talisman of this planet, to to a dream journey to this planet and so on.

V 2. Individual

In the horoscope, the 2nd house represents possessions and therefore one's relationship to money. Depending on which planets are in this house, one has a different relationship to money. The dynamics that shape one's relationship to money can be seen in the aspects that the planets in the 2nd house have to other planets – especially the squares, quincunxes and semisextiles are important in this context and sometimes also the oppositions.

The people who have a planet in the 2nd house that has a square, a quincunx, a semisextile or an opposition, have with some probability a "money theme". However, money can also play a role in other astrological constellations.

- In a **square**, there are two planets that must leave each other free. The square separates two things like a tent pole. Both planets must be able to unfold independently of each other.

- With a **quincunx** there has to be tidying up again and again. Every time something happens that belongs to the themes corresponding to the two planets linked by the quincunx, you have to reorient yourself, realign your course, incorporate the new.

- With a **semi-sextile**, there is always a tendency to move forward – always in the direction of the house sequence, that is, from the 2nd house into the 3rd to the 4th house and so on. In this case, the money in the 2nd house is not "safe", but tends to flow elsewhere …

- With an **opposition**, one must learn to swing back and forth between the two planets at either end of the opposition. This is a constant alternation between the 2nd house and probably the 8th house, that is, between eating and excreting food, between harmonizing and criticizing, between making money and spending money, etc. Ultimately, this is a life-enhancing rhythm.

It is beneficial, as everywhere in magic, to get to know one's own character and style and to behave according to it: Some people are sprinters, others marathon runners … and some get rich by speculating in stocks, while others prefer fixed-income securities with a short remaining term …

In recognizing one's own style, one's own horoscope can be of great help.

VI Money Magic and Chakra System

In order to relate money-magic to the chakra system, one must formulate the need for money somewhat more generally as a "desire to have what one needs."

The basic structure of the chakra system is simple: from identity to experience. This is found as radiating outward from the center in the heart chakra to the root chakra and the crown chakra.

The dynamics of the chakras		
Dynamics	*Chakra*	
identity	heart chakra	
general need	solar plexus	throat chakra
concrete desire	hara	third eye
experience	root chakra	crown chakra

When these chakras, i.e. the "life force organs" of the human being, can work unhindered, the person in question will radiate from the heart chara outwards – he radiates that, what he is. Then he is firmly anchored in his heart chakra.

However, if there are blockages in the life force body, areas of life force congestion and areas of life force deficiency will arise. Depending on where the congestion is, different imprints of character arise. The three basic whole qualities in the three pairs of chakras are:

The qualities of the chakras			
Dynamics	*Chakra*		*Quality*
identity	heart chakra		
general need	solar plexus	throat chakra	self-love
concrete desire	hara	third eye	power
experience	root chakra	crown chakra	abundance

The money theme is apparently centered in the two outer chakras, which stand for abundance.

Unfortunately, these three basic qualities can be disturbed in such a way that three sources of suffering arise from them:

The qualities and disturbances of the chakras				
Dynamics	**_Chakra_**		**_Quality_**	
			whole	_disturbed_
identity	heart chakra			
general need	solar plexus	throat chakra	self-love	self-doubt
concrete desire	hara	third eye	power	violence
experience	root chakra	crown chakra	abundance	lack

When these three basic qualities are disturbed, polarization occurs – one pole becomes louder and louder, the other pole becomes quieter and quieter:

The disturbances of the chakras					
Dynamics	**_Energy congestion in:_**	**_Quality_**			
		whole	_disturbed_		
			suffering	_"loud"_	_"quiet"_
identity	heart chakra				
general need	solar plexus	self-love	self-doubt	star	
	throat chakra				fan
concrete wish	hara	power	violence	perpetrator	
	third eye				victim
experience	root chakra	abundance	lack	addict	
	crown chakra				ascetic

One often encounters the three "loud" qualities together. Also the three "quiet" qualities are seen as a unity:

- The addict becomes the perpetrater and attracts all attention to himself (star).

- The ascetic feels like a victim and strives for an ideal (fan).

The three "loud" qualities occur when there is a life force congestion in one of the three lower chakras; the "quiet" qualities occur when there is a life force congestion in the three upper chakras.

The money theme has a different quality in these two basic types:

- The addict/perpetrator/star snatches everything and can never get enough, yet continues to live in lack.

- The ascetic/sacrificer/fan renounces more and more and hopes for a redemption in the future and also lives on in lack.

A money spell performed by these two basic types would consequently have a quite different approach:

- The addict/perpetrator/star seizes by magic out of his own power every-thing he wants and can grab. He tends to be the ritual type and the dominant power magician.

- The ascetic/sacrificer/fan asks a higher authority, usually the gods, for help and alms and in extreme cases for a reward in the hereafter. He tends to be the meditation type and the submissive mystic.

Both attitudes are extremes:

The two extremes	
addict/perpetrator/star	*ascetic/victim/fan*
"loud"	"quiet"
life force congestion in the three lower chakras	life force congestion in the three upper chakras
lack of life force in the three upper chakras	lack of life force in the three lower chakras
he sees himself completely on his own (alone)	he sees himself as a part of the "big one" (a part of the whole)
the whole world is his opponent	he is on the "right side"
he looks for salvation in his own power	he looks for salvation on the outside
exaggerated, short-sighted egoism	exaggerated, short-sighted altruism
asserts himself	holds back himself
pushes himself into the foreground	stays in the background
etc.	etc.

If one acts from one of these two extremes, the fruits of one's actions will also have that quality. Acting from an extreme can certainly bear fruit (an addict, for example, gets addictive substance), but the question is whether one can achieve a happy state when acting from an extreme (the addict does not become happy by his addictive substance).

In any case, when acting out of lack, violence and self-doubt, one will not find fullness, power and self-love. In order to arrive at these three whole qualities, one will have to deal with the causes of one's polarization:

- Why has one become an addict or an ascetic (both of which live in lack)?

- Why has one become a perpetrator or a victim (both of which live in violence)?

- Why has one become a star or a fan (both of which live in self-doubt)?

Both extremes cannot exist without their antithesis, and they know their antithesis intimately:

- Every greedy addict also carries a renouncing ascetic inside himself.
- Every renouncing ascetic also carries a greedy addict inside himself.

- Every aggressive perpetrator also carries a fearful victim inside himself.
- Every fearful victim also carries a aggressive perpetrator inside himself.

- Every megalomaniac star also carries a fan with inferiority complex inside himself.
- Every fan with inferiority complex also carries a megalomaniac star inside himself.

For the attainment of fullness, power and self-love, it will be necessary to find in oneself the opposite pole to one's own extreme behavior and to unite the hitherto lived extreme with the feared counter-extreme, to dissolve both and to rediscover the wholesome form of the subject in question:

- From the disturbance of fullness arises lack, which produces the two extreme behaviors of the addict and the ascetic, who can only return to fullness by dissolving their polarization.

- From the disturbance of power arises violence, which produces the two extreme behaviors of the perpetrator and the victim, who can only return to power by dissolving their polarization.

- From the disturbance of self-love arises self-doubt, which produces the two extreme behaviors of the star and the fan, which can only return to self-love through the dissolution of their polarization.

Now, it is clearly easier to describe these three possible polarizations than to resolve them. A first step is to recognize these polarizations within oneself and to see how they shape one's own life, including one's own relationship to money.

Today, money is the symbolic image of wealth, power and fame – which is all too often confused with abundance, power and self-love.

- Wealth is the term in which the addict and the ascetic think;

- Power is the term in which the perpetrator and the victim think; and

- Fame is the term in which the star and the fan think.

One can take a second step in a rather simple way. It is, in a way, a "mini family constellation" – similar to the constellation already described, where one person embodies the money and the other person embodies the "money seeker."

In this mini constellation, you place three sheets of paper next to each other on the floor and write "addict" and "ascetic" on the two outer ones and "abundance" on the middle one. Then you stand first on one of the two outer sheets, then on the other outer sheet and lastly on the middle sheet of paper, and look how these positions feel.

In this way you may feel this three states more clearly than if you would only think about them.

If you want, you can give an imagined hand to each of the two outer states while standing in the center. Then you may see if they want to return to the center, i.e. to the whole state.

In this way one can already get a feeling for the quality of fullness and also take a first step in the direction of fullness.

If one wishes, one can also say aloud, standing on the middle sheet of paper, that one will return to this state. The presence of a second person as a witness is extremely beneficial – the witness grounds the decision.

This mini constellation can also be done with "perpetrator", "victim" and "power" as well as with "star", "fan" and "self-love".

These two other themes can also be relevant for one's own relationship to money – if one sees money primarily as a means of power (perpetrator/victim) or as an expression of prestige (star/fan).

One can also try a third step. Since the three polarities are linked to the three pairs of chakras, one can also try to change this inner polarization on the life force level.

The method here is quite simple: one directs life force into the chakra that has a life force deficiency. For this purpose, one can use a two-word mantra as in the already described mantra meditation.

As the first word (source) a god of abundance or the name of one's own soul (or simply "my soul" or "soul") would be appropriate.

As the second word (aim), depending on the chakra, "abundance", "power" or "self-love" (or briefly "love") could be used.

This results in the following mantra meditations:

Mantra-Meditation				
Extreme	Chakra		Guiding one's breath into the following chakra:	Mantra
	Life force congestion	Life force deficiency		
addictive	root chakra	crown chakra	crown chakra	Soul – Fullness
ascetic	crown chakra	root chakra	root chakra	
perpetrater	hara	third eye	third eye	Soul – Power
victim	third eye	hara	hara	
star	solar plexus	throat chakra	throat chakra	Soul – Love
fan	throat chakra	solar plexus	solar plexus	

When inhaling, one speaks inwardly "soul" and imagines directing the life force (light) into the chakra in question;

and when exhaling, one inwardly speaks the second word ("fullness", "power" or "love") and imagines that in the chakra in question the life force directed there is radiating brightly.

A very thorough method is generally the Kundalini meditation, because by this the life force in one's own body begins to flow again and thereby all areas of life force congestions and life force deficiency as well as the associated feelings become conscious.

The chakras are located in the following places in the body:

- Crown chakra: at the top of the head.
- Third Eye: between the eyebrows
- Throat chakra: in the middle of the neck
- Heart chakra: in the middle of the chest
- Solar plexus: between sternum and navel
- Hara: four finger widths below the navel
- Root chakra: between genitals and anus

VII Money ... is that all?

A money spell does not stand isolated in one's life – it is a part of one's whole life situation. Therefore, it is also beneficial for the money theme to look at one's overall situation. A money spell will be more effective if it is performed as part of a comprehensive reorientation.

One can also visualize abundance, which is often reduced to the possession of money, in a more differentiated way using the four elements and the quintessence:

- Earth   = thriving prosperity
- Water   = love, closeness
- Air   = truth, knowledge
- Fire   = strength, health
- Light   = radiating out of ones's identity

The first four of these five forms of abundance are only "round" together. They spring from the fifth form of fullness, from the radiance of one's identity, which corresponds to the quintessence.

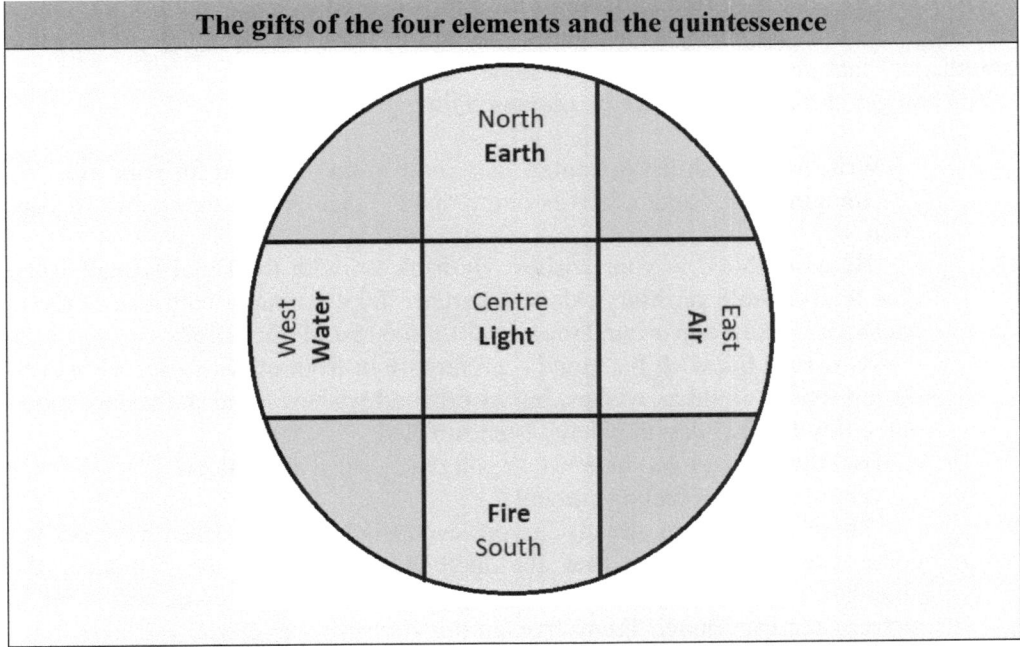

The gifts of the four elements and the quintessence

27

In order to arrive at a more comprehensive blueprint for one's own future, one can ask oneself the following questions, for example:

- What does money mean to me?
- What is my relationship to abundance?
- What is essential in my life?
- Why do I have too little money?
- Is it being taken away from me?
- Do I earn too little?
- Am I helping to finance my drug-addicted boyfriend?
- Am I the sole breadwinner in a shared apartment?
- What is my parents' relationship to money?
- Do I have money, but do I need more?
- Does money mean to me that I have a lot of prestrige?
- Do I live in the place where I want to live?
- Do I live with the people I want to be with?

There are many more questions like these, but it is best to see for yourself which questions are important to you.

The ultimate goal is to find a vision of the life you want to live – but not the image of a land of milk and honey as a counter-reaction to lack, but the image of "organic abundance" that makes the heart chakra shine.

You can get closer to this image by playing a little game:

- Write a gift wish list to Santa Claus about what you want for your life.
- Imagine that Santa Claus is omnipotent – then add more wishes to your wish list.
- Be uninhibited in your wishes: To drink tea with the Dalai Lama? To be able to fly? Walk on Mars? Have a harem? Take a money bath like Scrooge McDuck? Take a trip around the world for the rest of your life?
- Now read the wish list aloud – preferably in front of witnesses. However, do not read it aloud as wishes, but as fulfilled wishes. Read the wishes aloud and enjoy the fact that they have been fulfilled.
- Feel the feelings you have when you read your wishes aloud.
- Where are these feelings in you?
- These feelings are already in you, even though your wishes have not yet come true. This means that the happiness, the grin, the radiance, the abundance are already there – they are in your heart chakra and want to express and experience themselves in this life.

You don't need anything outside to be happy – happiness is already there in your own heart, looking for opportunities outside to express itself.

Of course, this game works best if you don't know all the steps of this game in advance, but go through it step by step – which is hard to do in a book, though. But you may play this game with others who don't know this game yet.

The essential experience that this game conveys is the rediscovery of one's own heart chakra: "I am not an empty vessel that needs to be filled from the outside – I am a cornucopia whose fullness wants to flow into the world."

This realization is ultimately the healing of the experience of lack and the feeling of lack. By rediscovering this inner source of the heart chakra, one's perspective changes, as vividly described in the book "Conversations with God": "Every situation is an opportunity to express who I am."

The addict and the ascetic, the perpetrator and the victim, the star and the fan all live in the image of an overpowering world in which they cannot be who they are. They all need something from the world to become who they are. They all no longer see the actual dynamic: the radiance of identity in one's heart chakra, which becomes general impulses in the solar plexus and throat chakra, which then become concrete impulses in the hara and third eye, and which then finally lead to experiences in the root chakra and crown chakra.

Rediscovering the source of one's own radiance within oneself is the real cure for the need of money – simply because by this the image of abundance, power and self-love returns back to the place, where the image of lack, violence and self-doubt have dwelt for some time.

These three qualities of abundance, power and self-love are then no longer sought in the world, but they flow out of oneself.

Of course, this view of things can only be convincing when one has experienced it oneself …

VIII Gods

One can broaden the background for one's own money magic one step more and include the gods or the collective subconsciousness. What is meant by this can best be described with an example:

> From the hippie-movement the Jesus-People developed from about 1968, who put their life completely under the protection of Jesus.
>
> They meet in the morning and have a look on what they need that day and then pray together for it: food, a place to stay, a bicycle, some fare, etc. By the evening, the members of the group have received all these things as a gift from someone.
>
> It is quite possible to live in this way.

The striking element about this particular form of money magic is the complete trust in a deity – in this case Jesus. This principle is also found among Krishna followers, Hindu mendicant monks, Buddhists, and others.

This trust causes a one-pointedness, which is also known from magic. It is found, for example, in the consecration of talismans or in the concentration on a sigil. There is a difference of the one-pointedness in magic compared to the trust of the groups which rely on a deity: the one-pointedness of trust in a deity is constantly there in one's life as a background – the one-pointedness has become a basic attitude. In magic, on the other hand, one-pointedness is only there for moments or for short periods of time.

Because of their constant one-pointedness, it is hardly possible to talk rationally with these people about their worldview – but they achieve what they want. And that is usually the more important point …

These people also have the deep conviction to act right. This makes them largely unassailable.

> It is not even necessary to trust in a particular deity – one can also trust in life.
>
> After I started my own business as a writer and consultant, my old existential fears came to the surface quite violently. I was able to calm down a bit with the fact that it is not so easy to die of poverty in Germany, but the image of starving and freezing to death under a bridge at some point simply could not be calmed down.
>
> One day I realized that I simply need a security, that it simply doesn't work for me without it. Then I spontaneously decided to trust "those up there" (my

soul, the gods, God, etc.). This was not a realization, not a planned action – this was a spontaneous decision. It came from the very inside and was one hundred percent, without any reservation.

Since then I have been supported by "those up there" – meanwhile for more then 15 years.

This attitude does not mean that you are all-powerful, that you get everything you want – but it means that you get everything you need and what is good for you.

Accepting changes in one's life is also a great help to this attitude: when one no longer clings to anything, space is made for abundance …

In the years that I wrote the 87 books on the Germanic gods, I sometimes had no money to pay my rent. In these cases I inwardly told the Germanic gods that I needed money and that otherwise I could not finish the books about them.

Apparently they thought that these books should be written, because I always received money after a short time – in one case, for example, a check about 500€ from a man whom I had helped a year earlier, by means of Feng Shui, to sell a property that he had wanted to get rid of for over 20 years. This man suddenly had the idea that he wanted to give me a larger amount for my help.

If "they up there" should ever be of the opinion that I should do something else than writing and consulting, then I will just do something else … it will then be something that enriches me even more than what I am currently doing.

This attitude of complete one-pointedness, in which there is no more doubt, uncertainty, wavering, skepticism and the like, leads also generally to the "extraordinary magic" like materializations, levitations and the like.

IX Do what you want

One can summarize the previous considerations in a simple way:

- Know yourself.
- Trust in life.
- Be courageous.
- Radiate who you are.
- Take the first step in the right direction.
- Do what you want – then prosperity will follow by itself.

X   Magic instead of market economy

The principle of "trust in life" has so far only been applied and lived by individuals and religious groups. What would happen if the whole mankind would apply this principle? What would change then? What can be said about such a form of living together?

- The trust in life or in the gods would create a fundamentally different foundation than is usual today.

- This trust, i.e. the "being borne by the whole" would be supplemented by a comprehensive responsibility, i.e. by a "bearing the whole". This is what is needed today in political, economic and ecological terms.

- Trust in the whole and responsibility for the whole would give rise to a world view and, above all, to an attitude to life and a way of behaving that is no longer the togetherness and antagonism of individual beings, but a continuum.
This continuum becomes more and more clear also in today's physics: There is the one "something" which can appear as space, time, energy and matter.

- Identity will then be rooted in the awareness of one's own quality and no longer in the demarcation against the "other".
This is the state of the enlightened that Buddha describes: boundless equanimity, boundless mercy, boundless love and boundless joy.

- Humanity will conceive of itself as a family because of this continuum. The economic-political aspect is already evident today as globalization.

- An essential step of development will be to reconcile individuality and globalization: Everyone is a part of the whole – every person is a part of humanity and indissolubly connected with it. Therefore, the appreciation of one's own individuality and the appreciation of the individuality of others belong together.
This does not mean that there will be no more conflicts, but only that they will be solved from a different point of view.

- The individual subconsciousness will be seen as an integral part of the collective subconsciousness. The individual subconscious is firmly connected to the collective subconscious through telepathy and telekinesis.

Therefore, desires borne of trust and responsibility can direct "chance." These types of desires can coordinate people's actions and direct the flow of goods.

Trust and responsibility enable a conscious connection to the collective subconsciousness – or to the gods, if this designation is preferred.

Trust and responsibility arise from the perception of the connection of the individual through telepathy and telekinesis with the whole.

Living in this consciousness and using this "being a part of the whole" is magic on a grand scale – and "extraordinary magic".

So far there are descriptions of it only in science fiction novels, where such societies appear as the "Planet of the Wise" and the like.

- Such a form of economy is not based on the lack-based consciousness, but on the abundance-based consciousness. Since in such an economic system things will no longer come to those who can pay most for these things, but to those who need them most urgently and have the greatest benefit by them, the total benefit of this kind of goods distribution will be much greater than today.

The distribution of goods by magic sounds utopian, but it is feasible – and it is effective.

One can begin with it also as an individual – I live since more than 15 years only from "donations". I give to the world what I like to give, and receive from the world what I need. Bartering with or without money is ultimately not an effective commodity distribution mechanism. If you always give to those who need it most and don't ask for anything in return, things will be distributed more meaningfully.

There are people who can give me nothing in return, some can give just a little, some a bit more, some plenty – and there are even people who give me a monthly donation, though I'm not doing anything for them.

- The trust and responsibility will also dissolve the money fixation, so that one can produce reasonable things again: Goods that are as durable as possible and have as little impact on the environment as possible.

The basic principle in this form of economy is "cooperation instead of competition". In the market economy there are unemployed people looking for work, there is capital, there are raw materials and there is knowledge – but the system is incapable of coordinating these things in such a way that everyone gets what they need …

Here another form of coordination is needed than the "competition for money" – this comprises two things:

1. If you produce more enduring products, you will maybe need double the amount of work and material, but if the products endure eight times as long as other products, you need in the long term only a quarter of the material and work. This would have the effect, that people wouldn't need to work eight hours a day but only two hours.

For this, of course, a reasonable distribution of work and money would be needed – just competition would not do …

2. If the overall view and the collective subconsciousness would be used by all, everyone would send out their wihses telepathically and receive some time later most of the things they need.

This is an economy based on wishes in trust and responsibility – on "one-directed wishes" … a "magical economy" …

Each individual can start with this by using the "one-directed money magic" that arises from the radiance of the heart chakra.

This outline of a future economic system does not at all mean that everyone must act in the same way – it is still necessary for everyone to find their own style in such a system.

It is also not necessary to "believe" in this system, because it will emerge by itself when enough people have discovered this "one-directed wishing" for themselves and apply it. Out of the egoism of the individuals this more meaningful system of economy will develop, if this egoism of the individuums is connected with expertise, insight and farsightedness – and magic.

The globalization needs no suppression of the egoism, but only a far-sighted egoism which overlooks the consequences of one's own actions – and which has the courage to try out new possibilities.

Money-magic is a good approach to this, if one does not stop at the first small successes, but curiously and courageously explores further and further how one can free the abundance in one's own life again.

XI Invocations

The following texts are not traditional texts, but self-penned "functional poetry" that have as many different forms as possible.

They are meant to help with the money rituals – they can be used as they are here, but they can just as well be changed, shortened or extended. Perhaps they will inspire you to write your own invocations and the like. The following verses are intended ro be only a starting help …

to Freyr

Freyr's friend, grant me fullness,
peace and full fields;
descendant of Njörd of Noatun,
for food, for fare I seek.

Spouse of Gefiun, you joyful of gifts,
give me money and goods and profit;
Wane of Wanaheim, wealth preserver,
grant me wll-being through the ages!

to Zeus

Thunder-bearer, mighty one, you king of Olympus,
your clouds send the field-fertilizing rain,
the cattle-pleasing wetness over the wine-rich Arcadia
the grain-treasure-laden Hellas, over the ship-borne sea;

Send me also tasty food for my table,
a house and a garden for my many-headed family,
battle-decider, helmet-crowned, Athena's father,
Hera's husband, Lord of Gods, let me prosper!

to Auriel

Auriel, Angel of the Northern Light Land
You hold a part of the multicolored ribbon,
that weaves the four forms of abundance –
full of gratitude.

Auriel, messenger of the fields, meadows and mountains,
Send me the gifts of your dwarves,
Give me what brings me prosperity,
so that my heart sings with joy!

to Lakshmi

Lakshmi, loving protector of Surya,
goddess of beauty and wife of kings,
give us abundance, pour rain on the fields,
expand our hearts in love for You.

Mixer of the golden Soma potion,
mother, your milk nourishes all people,
all animals, all plants, all beings,
You are the wealth – inside and outside!

to Enki

Enki, you make the grass green on the pastures,
Enki, you make the grain sprout in the fields;
Enki, you are the earth beneath our feet,
Enki, you are the ground under the hooves of our cattle.

Enki, you are the mountain that touches the sky,
Enki, you are the tower that greets the clouds;
Enki, you are the source of abundance,
Enki, you are the gate of prosperity!

to Geb

Geb, god of the earth, Ma'at is your essence,
Spouse of the sky, Ma'at is your fruit,
full of Ma'at is your gaze upon us –
Ma'at is the rightness in all things.

Geb, thou bearest the air-god Shu in Ma'at,
thou formest the plants in Ma'at,
thou givest the animals Ma'at in abundance –
Ma'at is the rightness in my heart.

to Iktomi

Iktomi, spider man, show me a way to abundance,
show me my totem pole, my animal, my soul;
you know all the hidden ways, the lists,
and all secrets – you are the Far Wandered One.

Connect me with the world, thou inventor of all that is new,
show me the old, the mother I seek,
you surely know the sweat lodge way to her
and all hidden treasures – you have seen much.

to Jupiter

Jupiter, planet of abundance in my horoscope,
open your gates for me, that I may come to you,
that your fullness flows to me, gives me wisdom,
that I may see who I am – and what makes me happy!

Jupiter, teach me to give freedom to my square,
to let the quincunx change and delight me,
to give the semisextile room to grow,
and to swing in opposition – and all this in joyful abundance!

XII   A Ritual of Abundance

In almost all people who explore and use ritual magic, the same effect shows up:

- First one uses simple traditional rituals;
- then the more complex traditional rituals;
- then the first simple rituals are composed by oneself;
- these rituals become more and more complex as time goes by;
- the intensity of the rituals increases and they become simpler again;
- the rituals become simple gestures;
- an inner attitude finally takes the place of the rituals.

The ritual presented in the following is depicted on the basis of this developmental arc until it finally loses all form and can become an attitude in life:

Part   1   serves the contact to the four elements and the quintessence.
Part 2-3   are elements used in the actual ritual.
Part 4-6   are the three parts of the abundance ritual.
Part   7   is the reduction of the ritual to its essential core.
Part 8-9   is the attitude in life that can be found by this ritual.

XII 1.   Dream Journey to the Elements

The first preparation is quite simple. It consists of five dream journeys – one each into the elements of earth, water, air and fire, and into the quintessence, or light. One can align in these elemental dream journeys in three different ways:

- either simply look at what you see,
- or look for the most important thing
- or ask an elemental deity or the elemental archangel to appear.

These dream journeys serve to "bring alive" the elements. If you already have a lot of experience with the Elements, you can skip this step.

As a gateway for the dream journeys you can use the symbols from the following list. In the first row there are the Indian Tattwa symbols; in the second row there are the alchemical symbols. In the third row there is another symbol of the centre, that is known both from India and from the Occident.

The symbols of the elements				
Light	*Fire*	*Water*	*Air*	*Earth*
black egg	red triangle	silver crescent	blue circle	yellow square

XII 2. Cabbalistic Cross

The cabbalistic cross has several functions: It is a sign of blessing, a sign of protection, and it can be used in rituals as a punctuation mark, so to speak, as a paragraph, a comma, and a semicolon to delineate individual parts of rituals.

The cabbalistic cross refers to the sephiroth (areas) of the cabbalistic tree of life.

The Cabbalistic Cross

Words (Aramaic)	Translation	Gesture
Ateh	Yours is	the left hand comes down from above and touches the forehead with the fingertips
Malkuth	the kingdom	the left hand draws the line that began above the head, further down until the hand points to a point below the feet, marking the vertical bar
ve-Geburah	and the power	the fingertips of the left hand touch the right shoulder
ve-Gedulah	and the glory	the fingertips of the left hand go over to the left shoulder and touch it, thereby drawing the crossbeam of the cross
le-Olam, Amen.	forever, amen.	both hands are folded in front of the chest, symbolically connecting the two beams, imagining a red rose at the point of intersection.

XII 3.   Lesser Pentagram Ritual

Since the pentagram ritual is a component of the ritual presented in sections XI. 5. to XI 7. it is useful to first practice this ritual for a while until it becomes familiar to one.

On the one hand, this ritual creates a protective space and, on the other hand, it charges this space with life force. It can therefore be used in many ways in magic.

Cabbalistic cross: *"Ateh Malkuth ve-Geburah ve-Gedulah le-Olam Amen."*

With the index and middle fingers of the right hand, indicate the drawing of the circle on the ground, imagining the circle – repeat twice; each time the circle becomes clearer.

Draw with the hand (gesture and imagination) the eastern pentagram (an upright pentagram with one point pointing upwards and two points pointing

41

downwards; one starts from the bottom left to the top center, further to the bottom right, to the center left, horizontally to the center right, to the bottom left). Hold your hand in the center of the imagined pentagram and chant, *"Yod-He-Vau-He"* (Element Air);

In the same way, draw the southern pentagram and chant *"Adonai"* (element of fire).

In the same way, draw the western pentagram and chant *"Eheieh"* (element of water).

In the same way, draw the northern pentagram and chant *"Agla"* (Element Earth).

Stand in the cross posture (arms stretched out to both sides) facing east and speak and imagine:
"In front of me Raphael (yellow and partly violet archangel of the air, holding a sword, in the background clouds),
behind me Gabriel (blue and partly orange archangel of water, holding a chalice, in the background the sea),
to my right hand Michael (red and partly green archangel of fire, holding a staff, in the background flames),
to my left hand Auriel (reddish brown and partly lemonyellow, olive-green and black archangel of the earth, holding a coin, in the background fields, pastures and forests),
I am standing in the middle of the circle (strengthen the imagination of the circle),
around me are flaming pentagrams (the four elements),
and above me radiates the six-pointed star (hexagram = symbol of the seven planets with the sun in the center)."

Cabbalistic cross: *"Ateh Malkuth ve-Geburah ve-Gedulah le-Olam Amen."*

XII 4. First Ritual: Ideal and Shadow

If one has little experience in ritual magic, it is advisable to perform the following three rituals (XI 4., XI 5. and XI 6.) individually on different days. If one is already skilled in ritual magic, they can be performed as a single, somewhat complex ritual.

In general, it is beneficial to perform important rituals on a full moon – the tension is greater and transformations are easier to achieve.

The goal of the first part of this three-part ritual is to dissolve the two polarized extremes (addict and ascetic) into which the image of abundance has broken apart, and to recover the wholesome image of abundance.

It is also possible that one does not find such extremes because one has already healed this issue – or this polarization has never occurred.

The extremes are both not the whole state, but just two opposite deviations. To make this clearer, here are a few examples:

Polarization and center		
too little ("quiet")	*center*	*too much ("loud")*
poor beggar	have what you need	rich king
loneliness	love	harem
powerlessness	power	might
fasting	enjoy food	gluttony
silence	talk	solo entertainer

All texts in this rituals are suggestions. If necessary, they should be shortened, expanded or reshaped so that you feel comfortable with them. You can also rewrite them completely, change them in any way or simply improvise. It is also important that the texts have a style that appeals to you. The texts in this ritual have been written in much the same style as the "Golden Dawn" rituals.

The following suggested texts serve to make clear what is happening in the ritual.

1. The ritual place is defined, consecrated and charged with life force by the pentagram ritual.

2. One stands facing east. If one is right-handed, one extends the right arm (otherwise the left arm) to the front and forms the hand into a flat bowl.

> *"Air in me,*
> *my thinking, my cognition, my speaking –*
> *that which I strive for with effort,*
> *may appear in my right hand."*

One looks at what one can perceive in one's hand. One feels into what one sees.

Now you stretch out your left arm and hand (if you are right-handed) to the front and form a shallow bowl with your hand.

> *"Air in me,*
> *my thinking, my recognizing, my speaking –*
> *that which I avoid with effort,*
> *may appear in my left hand."*

One looks again what one can perceive in one's hand. One feels into what one sees.

Now you slowly bring your hands together and put them together so that between the palms there is a hollow space in which the air-ideal and the air-shadow are located. Since both are two opposites, two polar extremes, they begin to fight and destroy each other.

> *"Serpent of the Earth-Fire,*
> *Kundalini,*
> *bring life force into the ideal and the shadow of my air,*
> *dissolve the rigid, sorrowful opposition within me."*

You wait until you notice between the palms of your hands the warmth that comes from the serpent and the dissolution of the opposites.

> *"Eagle of Light,*
> *Celestial Messenger,*
> *bring the memory of the true form back into my air,*
> *let the air be reborn in me."*

When you feel that the new form of air has come into being, you open your hands and hold them side by side so that the two palms form a shallow bowl. You look at what you now see on your palms.

Then you take your own transformed, "de-polarized" and healed air back into yourself by placing your two palms with the healed air on your heart chakra.

3. now perform the same in the south with the fire. Since the actions are the same, here are only the spoken texts are given:

"Fire in me,
my actions, my fighting, my dancing –
that which I strive for with effort,
may appear in my right hand."

"Fire in me,
my acting, my fighting, my dancing –
that which I avoid with effort,
may appear in my left hand."

"Serpent of the Earth-Fire,
Kundalini,
bring life force to the ideal and the shadow of my fire,
dissolve the rigid, sorrowful opposition within me."

"Eagle of Light,
Celestial Messenger,
bring the memory of the true form back into my fire,
let the fire be reborn in me."

4. Now perform the same in the west with the water:

"Water in me,
my loving, my longing, my feeling –
that which I strive for with effort,
may appear in my right hand."

"Fire in me,
my loving, my longing, my feeling –
that which I avoid with effort,
may appear in my left hand."

"Serpent of the Earth-Fire,
Kundalini,
bring life force to the ideal and the shadow of my water,
dissolve the rigid, sorrowful opposition in me."

"Eagle of Light,
Celestial Messenger,
bring the memory of the true form back into my water,
let the water be reborn in me."

5. Now perform the same in the north with the earth:

"Earth in me,
my forming, my grasping, my working –
that which I strive for with effort,
may appear in my right hand."

"Earth in me,
my forming, my grasping, my working –
that which I avoid with effort,
may appear in my left hand."

"Serpent of the Earth-Fire,
Kundalini,
bring life force to the ideal and the shadow of my earth,
dissolve the rigid, sorrowful opposition within me."

"Eagle of Light,
Celestial Messenger,
bring the memory of the true form back to my earth,
let the earth be reborn in me."

6. One stands in the center and faces east. One allows time to feel the four elements in the four directions and the changes within oneself.

7. one finishes the ritual with the pentagram ritual.

XII 5.   Second Ritual: The Archangels

This second part of the abundance ritual has the function to put the healing states of the four elements found in the first part into a larger context and to let them become a part of the general four elements. One's fire becomes part of the general fire, one's air becomes part of the general air, and so on. These four general elements appear as the four archangels who are called in the pentagram ritual.

Here the images in one's individual subconsciousness are connected with the archetypal images in the collective subconsciousness.

1. The ritual place is defined, consecrated and charged by the pentagram ritual with life force.

2. one stands in the east and looks at the Raphael the archangel of air. One makes a gesture with his arms and hands as if opening a two-part curtain and pushing it away to the left and right.

> *"Raphael, Archangel of the Air,*
> *open for me the Gate of the East,*
> *show me the air in the world,*
> *let me see that which enriches me."*

You stop for a while and see what you perceive.

You place both hands on your heart, reflect on the quality of the healed air within you, and then move both arms and hands forward in a gesture of opening yourself. In doing so, one imagines that one is opening one's own healed air to the general air.

> *"I open my air to the air in the world,*
> *my thinking, my knowing, my speaking –*
> *Raphael, let the air of the world blow through me,*
> *that I may be connected with all knowledge."*

You look at how this opening feels, what you perceive, what happens.

> *"Raphael, open to me the fullness of the air,*
> *direct the knowledge, the insight, the truth to me,*
> *help me to dissolve my limits*
> *and let my air become part of the wind."*

One feels again how this opening feels.

One sends out rays of light, threads of life force to the east, telepathically and telekinetically connecting one's air with the air in the world.

> *"Raphael, Archangel of the Temple of Air,*
> *let me dwell in Thy Sanctuary,*
> *become a breath in Your Air*
> *and enjoy Your Fullness."*

3. Now perform the same in the south with fire. Since the actions are the same, here are only the spoken texts given:

> *"Michael, Archangel of Fire,*
> *open for me the Gate of the South,*
> *show me the fire in the world,*
> *let me see that which enriches me."*

> *"I open my fire to the fire in the world,*
> *my acting, my fighting, my dancing –*
> *Michael, let the fire of the world flame through me,*
> *that I may be connected with all power."*

> *"Michael, open to me the fullness of the fire,*
> *direct the power, the enthusiasm, the desire to me,*
> *help me to dissolve my limits*
> *and let my flames become part of the fire."*

> *"Michael, Archangel of the Temple of Fire,*
> *let me dwell in Your Sanctuary,*
> *become a flame in Your Fire*
> *and enjoy Your Fullness."*

4. Now perform the same in the west with water:

> *"Gabriel, Archangel of Water,*
> *open for me the Gate of the West,*
> *show me the water in the world,*
> *let me see that which enriches me."*

"I open my water to the floods in the world,
my loving, my longing, my feeling –
Gabriel, let the waters of the world flow through me,
that I may be connected with all love."

"Gabriel, open to me the fullness of the waters,
direct the feelings, the sympathy, the love towards me,
help me to dissolve my boundaries
and let my water become part of the sea."

"Gabriel, Archangel of the Temple of Water,
let me dwell in Your Sanctuary,
become a drop in Your Waters
and enjoy Your Fullness."

5. Now perform the same in the north with earth.

"Auriel, Archangel of the Earth,
open for me the Gate of the North,
show me the earth in the world,
let me see that which enriches me."

"I open my earth to the earth in the world,
my forming, my grasping, my working –
Auriel, let the earth of the world fill me,
that I become connected with all earth."

"Auriel, open to me the fullness of the earth,
direct the prosperity, the thriving, the fruits to me,
help me to dissolve my boundaries
and let my earth become part of the earth."

"Auriel, Archangel of the Earth Temple,
let me dwell in Your Sanctuary,
become a crumb in Your Earth
and enjoy Your Fullness."

6. One stands in the center and faces east. One feels the four elements around oneself – and one feels oneself (as far as possible) as an integrated part of these elements.

7. You finish the ritual with the pentagram ritual.

XII 6.   Third Ritual: The Continuum

In the third part of this ritual the four elements become connected and unified – thus becoming light, the quintessence.

Maybe a contemplation about the connections between the four elements would be helpful before starting this part of the ritual:

> By burning ("fire") wood ("earth") becomes smoke ("air").
> By freezing water becomes ice ("earth")
> By heating ("fire") water becomes steam ("air").
> etc.
>
> Love ("water") may give strenght ("fire").
> Truth ("air") may give relaxation ("water").
> Strenght ("fire") may give thriving ("earth").
> etc.

1. The ritual place is defined, consecrated and charged by the pentagram ritual with life force.

2. One stands facing east toward Raphael and opens his arms in a receiving gesture.

> *"Raphael, Wind of the World,*
> *I blow as a part of Thee within Thee,*
> *Your knowledge, Your movement, Your change*
> *are also in me."*

You turn around and stand with your back to the east. You raise your arms and hands first south to the fire (second line of the text), then west to the water (third line of the text), then north to the earth (forth line of the text).

> *"Raphael, Wind of the World,*
> *Your fullness flows to the fire in the south,*
> *Your fullness flows to the water in the west,*
> *Your fullness flows to the earth in the north."*

You continue to stand with your back to the east and raise your arms and hands toward the center.

> *"Raphael, Wind of the World,*
> *Your fullness flows into the center,*
> *into my heart, my soul, my source*
> *And shines in my thinking, cognizing, speaking."*

You go to the center, face east and place both hands on your heart chakra.

> *"Raphael, Wind of the World,*
> *You are in everything and in me;*
> *Raphael, Wind of the World,*
> *You are the fullness in my life."*

One remains like this for a while, enjoying the fullness.

3. now one performs the same in the south with fire:

> *"Michael, Fire of the World,*
> *I burn as a part of You in You,*
> *Your power, Your enthusiasm, Your desire*
> *are also in me."*

> *"Michael, Fire of the World,*
> *Your fullness flows to the water in the west,*
> *Your fullness flows to the earth in the north,*
> *Thy fullness flows to the air in the east."*

"Michael, Fire of the World,
your fullness flows to the center,
into my heart, my soul, my source
And shines in my loving, longing, feeling."

"Michael, Fire of the World,
You are in everything and in me;
Michael, Fire of the World,
You are the fullness in my life."

One remains like this for a while, enjoying the fullness.

4. Now one performs the same in the west with the water:

"Gabriel, Water of the World,
I flow as a part of You in You,
Your feeling, Your compassion, Your love,
are also in me."

"Gabriel, Water of the World,
Your fullness flows to the earth in the north,
Your fullness flows to the air in the east,
Thy fullness flows to the fire in the south."

"Gabriel, Water of the World,
your fullness flows to the center,
into my heart, my soul, my source
And shines in my loving, longing, feeling."

"Gabriel, Water of the World,
You are in everything and in me;
Gabriel, Water of the World,
You are the fullness in my life."

One remains like this for a while, enjoying the fullness.

5. Now one performs the same in the north with earth:

> *"Auriel, Earth of the World,*
> *I thrive as a part of You in You,*
> *Thy prosperity, Thy thriving, Thy fruits,*
> *are also in me."*

> *"Auriel, Earth of the World,*
> *Your fullness flows to the air in the east,*
> *Your fullness flows to the fire in the south,*
> *Thy fullness flows to the water in the west."*

> *"Auriel, Earth of the World,*
> *your fullness flows to the center,*
> *into my heart, my soul, my source*
> *And shines in my forming, grasping, working."*

> *"Auriel, Earth of the World,*
> *You are in everything and in me;*
> *Auriel, Earth of the World,*
> *Thou art the fullness in my life."*

One stays like this for a while, enjoying the fullness.

6. One goes to the center and feels the fullness of the four elements, which here in the center becomes one manifold fullness.

One puts both hands on one's heart chakra and feels the abundance within oneself – and the soul in one's own heart chakra as the center of this abundance, as the origin of one's own radiance.

When one has stood long enough with the abundance in and around oneself, one greets the abundance in the world and in oneself with an appropriate gesture to the east, south, west, north and center.

7. One ends the ritual with the pentagram ritual.

XII 7. The Heart of the Ritual

This detailed ritual can be condensed into a simple ritual. However, this simple ritual has depth and greater effect only when 1. the transformation of the two extremes, 2. the connection with the archangels, and 3. the merging of the four forms of fullness have been previously performed as a ritual or in dream journeys. The ritual presented in the following is therefore not a substitute for the individual steps described in sections XI. 4. to XI 6. but only their summary.

One can, of course, begin with this ritual and then, if necessary, perform the more detailed ritual. These rituals are not a panacea and also not the only correct ritual, but merely an aid in one's own healing. Therefore, you should see if and how you want to use them – everyone knows that best himself …

1. The ritual place is defined, consecrated and charged by the pentagram ritual with life force.

2. You stand in the middle and hold your two hands in front of you and put your ideals in your right hand (for right-handed people) and your shadows in your left hand.

Then one puts both hands together and calls the earth-fire snake to dissolve the opposites. Also here and in the following parts of the ritual one describes with improvised words what one is doing.

Then one calls the sky-light eagle, that it reminds the dissolved opposites of their original form.

3. You stand in the center and open your arms to the four archangels and let your fire, air, water and earth connect with the fire, air, water and earth of the world – the four archangels become part of you and you become part of the four archangels.

4. one stands in the center and is connected with the four elements. One begins to take hold of the elements with appropriate movements as in a small dance, to mix them, to transform one into the other and to open oneself to this dance of the elements and their diversity and abundance.

5. One enjoys the abundance as long as one wants.

6. one ends the ritual with the pentagram ritual.

XII 8.   The Gesture

One can also combine this ritual into a simple sequence of movements that represent the parts of the ritual.

1. Place the hands on the heart chakra.

2. Hold the hands in front of you, place them together, wait and open them again.

3. Stretch the arms towards the archangels.

4. Place the hands on the heart chakra again.

5. Dance the Elements Dance, experiencing the diversity and unity of abundance.

6. Place the hands again on the heart chakra.

XII 9.   The Posture

The attitude and experience to be fostered by this ritual are trust in and responsibility for the world, experiencing oneself as an integrated part of the continuum, being attuned to unhindered self-expression, to the dance of life in fullness ...

English Books by Harry Eilenstein

- Living Magic (261 p.)	- Kundalini for Beginners
- The Synthesis of Physics and Magic (192 p.)	- Chakra-Magic for Beginners
- Astral Projection for Beginners (60 p.)	- Astrology for Beginners
- Invocations for Beginners (52 p.)	- Ritual Magic for Beginners
- Evocations for Beginners (62 p.)	- Mandalas for Beginners
- Auto-Movement for Beginners (60 p.)	- Love Magic for Beginners
- Elves for Beginners (56 p.)	- Magic Research for Beginners
- Hypnosis for Beginners (56 p.)	- Self-awareness for Beginners
- Money Magic for Beginners (60 p.)	- Symbolism of Numbers for Beginners
- Shamanism for Beginners (52 p.)	- Language of the Moon – for Beginners
- Crop Circles for Beginners (344 p.)	- Magic Chant for Beginners
- Number Symbolism for Beginners (64 p.)	- Prophecy for Beginners
	- Magic Objects for Beginners
These books will be puplished soon:	- Da'ath-Magic for Beginners
	- Feng Shui for Beginners
- Telepathy for Beginners	- Magic for Beginners – Anthology I
- Telepathy for Advanced Learners	- Magic for Beginners – Anthology II
- Telekinesis for Beginners	- Magic for Beginners – Anthology III
- Life Force for Beginners	- Magic for Beginners – Anthology IV
- Meditation for Beginners	

Bücher von Harry Eilenstein

Religion allgemein
- Die sieben Schritte des Lebens (428 S.)
- Muttergöttin und Schamanen (168 S.)
- Göbekli Tepe (472 S.)
- Die Göttin von Göbekli Tepe (144 S.)
- Totempfähle (440 S.)
- Christus (60 S.)
- Dakini (80 S.)
- Vajra (76 S.)

Ägypten
- Hathor und Re 1: Götter und Mythen im Alten Ägypten (432 S.)
- Hathor und Re 2: Die altägyptische Religion – Ursprünge, Kult und Magie (396 S.)
- Isis (508 S.)

Indogermanen
- Die Entwicklung der indogermanischen Religionen (700 S.)
- Wurzeln und Zweige der indogermanischen Religion (224 S.)

Germanen
- Die Götter der Germanen (87 Bände – siehe nächste Seite)
- Odin (300 S.)

Kelten
- Cernunnos (690 S.)
- Taliesin (228 S.)
- Der Kessel von Gundestrup (220 S.)
- Der Chiemsee-Kessel (76)

Psychologie
- Über die Freude (100 S.)
- Das Geheimnis des inneren Friedens (252 S.)
- Das Beziehungsmandala (52 S.)
- Gefühle und ihre Verwandlungen (404 S.)
- einsgerichtet (140 S.)
- Liebe und Eigenständigkeit (216 S.)
- Von innerer Fülle zu äußerem Gedeihen (52 S.)

Heilung
- Die Symbolik der Krankheiten (76 S.)

Kunst
- Herz des Tanzes – Tanz des Herzens (160 S.)

Drama
- König Athelstan (104 S.)

Bücher von Harry Eilenstein

„Magie für Anfänger"

- Telepathie für Anfänger (60 S.)
- Telepathie für Fortgeschrittene (52 S.)
- Telekinese für Anfänger (52 S.)
- Lebenskraft für Anfänger (60 S.)
- Meditation für Anfänger (56 S.)
- Kundalini für Anfänger (100 S.)
- Hypnose für Anfänger (56 S.)
- Auto-Movement für Anfänger (56 S.)
- Chakra-Magie für Anfänger (148 S.)
- Astralreisen für Anfänger (56 S.)
- Astrologie für Anfänger (120 S.)
- Ritual-Magie für Anfänger (56 S.)
- Mandalas für Anfänger (68 S.)
- Geldzauber für Anfänger (56 S.)
- Liebeszauber für Anfänger (52 S.)
- Invokationen für Anfänger (52 S.)
- Evokationen für Anfänger (60 S.)
- Elfen für Anfänger (56 S.)
- Magie-Forschung für Anfänger (140 S.)
- Selbsterkenntnis für Anfänger (52 S.)
- Zahlensymbolik für Anfänger (60 S.)
- Die Sprache des Mondes – für Anfänger (116 S.)
- Zaubergesänge für Anfänger (100 S.)
- Zukunftschau für Anfänger (60 S.)
- Schamanismus für Anfänger (52 S.)
- Magische Gegenstände für Anfänger (68 S.)
- Da'ath-Magie für Anfänger (64 S.)
- Kornkreise für Anfänger (348 S.)
- Feng Shui für Anfänger (96 S.)
- Magie für Anfänger – Sammelband I (696 S.)
- Magie für Anfänger – Sammelband II (664 S.)
- Magie für Anfänger – Sammelband III (580 S.)

„Traumreisen"

- Traumreisen zu Heilpflanzen (700 S.)

Magie

- Handbuch für Zauberlehrlinge (408 S.)
- Tarot (104 S.)
- Physik und Magie (184 S.)
- Die Synthese von Physik und Magie (200S.)
- Die Magie-Formel (156 S.)
- Krafttiere – Tiergöttinnen – Tiertänze (112 S.)
- Schwitzhütten (524 S.)
- Mythen und Magie der Harfe (116 S.)
- Magie heute – Berichte aus der Praxis (288 S.)

Meditation

- Der Lebenskraftkörper (230 S.)
- Die Chakren (100 S.)
- Das Chakren-System mit den Nebenchakren (296 S.)
- Organe und Chakren (64 S.)
- Die platonischen Körper in den Chakren (156 S.)
- Meditation (140 S.)
- Drachenfeuer (124 S.)
- Kundalini I (676 S.)
- Reinkarnation (156 S.)
- einsgerichtet (140 S.)

Astrologie

- Astrologie (496 S.)
- Photo-Astrologie (428 S.)
- Die astrologischen Aspekte (88 S.)
- Horoskop und Seele (120 S.)

Kabbala

- Kursus der praktischen Kabbala (150 S.)
- Eltern der Erde (450 S.)
- Blüten des Lebensbaumes:
    - Die Struktur des kabbalistischen Lebensbaumes (370 S.)
    - Der kabbalistische Lebensbaum als Forschungshilfsmittel (580 S.)
    - Der kabbalistische Lebensbaum als spirituelle Landkarte (520 S.)

Die Themen der 87 Bände der Reihe „Die Götter der Germanen"

1. Die Entwicklung der germanischen Religion
2. Lexikon der germanischen Religion
3. Der ursprüngliche Göttervater Tyr
4. Tyr in der Unterwelt: der Schmied Wieland
5. Tyr in der Unterwelt: der Riesenkönig Teil 1
6. Tyr in der Unterwelt: der Riesenkönig Teil 2
7. Tyr in der Unterwelt: der Zwergenkönig
8. Der Himmelswächter Heimdall
9. Der Sommergott Baldur
10. Der Meeresgott: Ägir, Hler und Njörd
11. Der Eibengott Ullr
12. Die Zwillingsgötter Alcis
13. Der neue Göttervater Odin Teil 1
14. Der neue Göttervater Odin Teil 2
15. Der Fruchtbarkeitsgott Freyr
16. Der Chaos-Gott Loki
17. Der Donnergott Thor
18. Der Priestergott Hönir
19. Die Göttersöhne
20. Die unbekannteren Götter
21. Die Göttermutter Frigg
22. Die Liebesgöttin: Freya und Menglöd
23. Die Erdgöttinnen
24. Die Korngöttin Sif
25. Die Apfel-Göttin Idun
26. Die Hügelgrab-Jenseitsgöttin Hel
27. Die Meeres-Jenseitsgöttin Ran
28. Die unbekannteren Jenseitsgöttinnen
29. Die unbekannteren Göttinnen
30. Die Nornen
31. Die Walküren
32. Die Zwerge
33. Der Urriese Ymir
34. Die Riesen
35. Die Riesinnen
36. Mythologische Wesen
37. Mythologische Priester und Priesterinnen
38. Sigurd/Siegfried
39. Helden und Göttersöhne
40. Die Symbolik der Vögel und Insekten
41. Die Symbolik der Schlangen, Drachen und Ungeheuer
42.a Die Symbolik der Herdentiere I
42.b Die Symbolik der Herdentiere II
43. Die Symbolik der Raubtiere
44. Die Symbolik der Wassertiere und sonstigen Tiere
45. Die Symbolik der Pflanzen
46. Die Symbolik der Farben
47. Die Symbolik der Zahlen
48. Die Symbolik von Sonne, Mond und Sternen
49.a Das Jenseits I – Das Hügelgrab
49.b Das Jenseits II – Der Jenseitsweg
50. Seelenvogel, Utiseta und Einweihung
51. Wiederzeugung und Wiedergeburt
52. Elemente der Kosmologie
53. Der Weltenbaum
54. Die Symbolik der Himmelsrichtungen und der Jahreszeiten
55.a Mythologische Motive I
55.b Mythologische Motive II
56. Der Tempel
57. Die Einrichtung des Tempels
58. Priesterin – Seherin – Zauberin – Hexe
59. Priester – Seher – Zauberer
60. Rituelle Kleidung und Schmuck
61. Skalden und Skaldinnen
62 Kriegerinnen und Ekstase-Krieger
63. Die Symbolik der Körperteile
64.a Magie und Ritual I
64.b Magie und Ritual II
64.c Magie und Ritual III
65. Gestaltwandlungen
66.a Magische Angriffs-Waffen
66.b Magische Verteidigungs-Waffen
67. Magische Werkzeuge und Gegenstände
68. Zaubersprüche
69. Göttermet
70. Zaubertränke
71. Träume, Omen und Orakel
72. Runen
73. Sozial-religiöse Rituale
74. Weisheiten und Sprichworte
75. Kenningar
76. Rätsel
77. Die vollständige Edda des Snorri Sturluson
78. Frühe Skaldenlieder
79.a Mythologische Sagas I
79.b Mythologische Sagas II
80. Hymnen an die germanischen Götter